Original title:
The Charm of the Chain

Copyright © 2025 Creative Arts Management OÜ
All rights reserved.

Author: Micah Sterling
ISBN HARDBACK: 978-1-80586-207-9
ISBN PAPERBACK: 978-1-80586-679-4

Links of Serendipity

In a trinket shop, I found a ring,
It pulled my finger—what a wild fling!
Now I trip and tumble, what a sync,
This little loop seems to love to wink.

Last week it linked my shoe to a stick,
And taught my heel a little magic trick.
With every hop, it dances, oh, so spry,
Leaving chaos giggling, oh me, oh my!

The Tangle of Shared Secrets

In whispers low, our secrets blend,
A garland of tales that twist and bend.
Like yarn in knots, it tickles the mind,
Laughter erupts, oh what will we find?

Each juicy story loops round a pole,
A jumbled mess, yet it fills my soul.
With every giggle, a twist of fate,
Our tangled truths join to celebrate.

Interlinked Souls in Celestial Dance

Stars above play a glorious tune,
With wobbly steps, we dance on the moon.
Funky and flailing, we trip in the night,
Our cosmic chain glimmers, what a sight!

As meteors whiz, we spin with delight,
In this wobbly waltz, we feel so light.
Gravity's grip can't hold back our cheer,
Interlinked giggles draw everyone near.

The Art of Tangled Journeys

Maps are for sissies, I'll go my own way,
With a twist and a turn, I'll wander and play.
Every wrong turn, a new laugh to share,
A tangled delight in the open air.

My suitcase is fighting a battle of sorts,
With socks interwoven and missing forks.
But each little mess leads me somewhere grand,
In this crazy trip, life's just unplanned!

Unity in Diversity

In a world filled with quirks and laughs,
We dance like ducks on a cold mountain path.
Pigs wear hats, and cats ride bikes,
Unity found in our joyful spikes.

From jellybeans to sour green peas,
Our differences are what spark the pleas.
With giggles shared over a cup of cheer,
Life's oddball charm is what we hold dear.

Signature of the Bound

Tangled in laughter with socks that don't match,
Bound by the stitches of a bizarre patch.
Writing our stories in crayons and glee,
Each scribble a note in our grand jubilee.

Frogs serenade while we munch on pie,
A symphony made of hiccups and sighs.
Signatures swirl in a love so profound,
Together, we fly with wings that astound!

Cadence of the Conjoined

Two left feet strike a rhythm so wild,
As we tango on rakes, oh, what a child!
Step on your toes, hop over the vine,
In this dance of flops, we gracefully shine.

With a twist and a shout, we aim for the sky,
Wobbling with joy as the birds fly by.
Our silly ballet, a sight quite divine,
A cadence of laughter, perfectly aligned.

Legacy of the Chapel

In a chapel of giggles beneath the moonlight,
We lay our plans for a snooze-fest delight.
A legacy formed in pillow fights grand,
With fluffy results we all understand.

The statues all grin at our late-night quests,
As we prank one another and take some rests.
A world of fun in sacred confine,
Where laughter's the mantra, and joy is the sign.

Embraced by the Circle

In a world where we all cling tight,
Round and round, much to our delight,
A loop of giggles, a twist of fate,
Link me to you; let's celebrate!

Bobbing heads like a linked parade,
Trip on laughter, don't be afraid,
Funky moves from one to the next,
In this dance, we're all perplexed!

Hold on tight, don't let it snap,
Silly bonds with a playful clap,
Each link a story, quirky and grand,
Let's frolic together, hand in hand!

Radiance of Relational Links

Shiny friends in a chaotic web,
Tangled tales, each one a drab,
A sparkle here, a wink right there,
With every twist, we show we care.

Juggling jokes and absurdity,
A tapestry of hilarity,
Slips and trips, a comic fail,
Yet under it all, we never bail.

Witty words and playful jives,
We're a crew where humor thrives,
In every loop, a grand old jest,
Creating bonds that stand the test!

Strength in the Tangle

In a knot of friends, we find our might,
A jumbled mess that feels just right,
Hiccups, laughs, we're all entwined,
Strength in chaos, so well-defined.

With every twist, a joke unfolds,
Witty banter never gets old,
We fumble, tumble, laugh it off,
In this tangle, we scoff and scoff!

Holding on through thick and thin,
Laughter ringing, we all win,
Each twist a reason to rejoice,
Together, we are a joyful voice!

Captivating Loops

Round and round the laughter flows,
Chasing tails like puppy shows,
In captivating circles, we embrace,
Every loop, a smiling face.

Flip-flop failures, that's our cue,
To dance and skip, just me and you,
Riding the wave of whimsy's reign,
In our dizzy world, we feel no pain.

Going in circles, what a sight,
Twists and turns bring pure delight,
So hold on tight; let's start the chase,
In this loop, we find our place!

Serenity in the Sturdy Links

In every clink, a giggle grows,
A dance of links, where laughter flows.
Wobbly charms upon my wrist,
They jingle loud, they can't resist.

A turtle joined my brassy show,
He scoots along, oh so slow.
With each bright bead, the fun expands,
In this parade, we're hand in hands.

The Symbiotic Whispers of Togetherness

Two peas in pods, we strut our stuff,
Who knew three links would be this tough?
They whisper secrets, silly and sly,
Armored buddies, reaching for the sky.

A twist, a turn, oh what a site,
We swing and sway, oh what delight!
Tangled tales of shiny glee,
Together bound, just you and me.

Links of Enchantment

A quirk in metal, a giggle's spark,
Every twist plays in the park.
With swaying charms that tickle toes,
They tell the tales only laughter knows.

In the sunshine, we gleam and gleefully shout,
Come see the colors, come check it out!
In jangling joy, we dance along,
These merry charms, our funny song.

Ties That Breathe

A stretch of chains, a snap of fun,
With winks and nudges, we come undone.
In every clasp, a heart-shaped glow,
The more we link, the more we know.

Bouncing links, they giggle and spin,
In sync we dance, we twirl and grin.
Oh what a mess, but what a catch,
Laughter's the key, it's quite a match.

The Beauty in Linked Destinies

In a world of quirky knots,
We dance in fumbles and lots.
A slip, a trip, but never a flaw,
Together we laugh, our friendship's raw.

Each twist and turn, a tale to share,
With laughter echoing in the air.
We're bound by goofs, a joyful spree,
In this tangled mess, just you and me.

Serpentine Shadows of Togetherness

Like shadows chasing in the sun,
We trip on paths, but still have fun.
With every stumble, a giggle erupts,
As tangled friends, we find our lucks.

In winding roads of silly fate,
We weave our laughter, life's first-rate.
Mismatched shoes and socks galore,
In this somersault, we explore.

The Magic of Intertwined Lives

A twist of fate, what could go wrong?
We sing our tune, a quirky song.
In every mix-up, a spark ignites,
Our jamboree of laugh-filled nights.

With hearts entwined, we pull and tug,
A mess of joy, like a warm snug.
In every hiccup, love's delight,
We twirl through life, a dazzling sight.

Rhythm of the Forged Comrades

Bound by silliness, we soar so high,
With silly dances that reach the sky.
Each clumsy step, a rhythm so sweet,
We stumble together, never face defeat.

In the forge of friendship, sparks do fly,
We laugh through tears, never asking why.
With quirky beats, we march as one,
In the symphony of fun, forever spun.

Unity in the Echoing Silence

In a room full of whispers,
A noisy sock parade,
They dance past the furniture,
In a jumbled charade.

Lurking socks take their chances,
On the edge of the floor,
Mismatched but full of antics,
Always ready for more.

Echoes of laughter tremble,
When odd socks don a hat,
They tumble down the hallway,
Who thought socks could do that?

Unity in sheer madness,
With each cheeky little grin,
Each pair brings silly stories,
Where the fun will begin.

Chains of Stardust and Wishes

A comet passed by quickly,
As wishes twinkled bright,
We caught them in the chaos,
In a bucket of starlight.

With dreams that chain together,
Like a jumble of threads,
We twirled and laughed like children,
Till we fell into our beds.

Each wish a glowing trellis,
Lifting spirits to the sky,
We giggle at our fate,
As we simply float by.

Though our hopes may tangle,
In a bizarre cosmic dance,
Each star links us like magic,
In a whimsical romance.

The Poetry of Interlapping Journeys

Two penguins on a journey,
With waddle and with flair,
They trip over their own feet,
And slide without a care.

Through icy realms of laughter,
Their paths entwined so sweet,
Each stumble tells a story,
In their snowy retreat.

They quack about their travels,
With tales of fish and cheer,
Adventures of mischief,
As the icebergs disappear.

Together through the chaos,
In their feathery attire,
These journeys blend in rhythm,
Like a dance on icy fire.

Forged in Fire, Bound by Trust

Two friends, a trio of socks,
On the clothesline do they swing,
They chat about the weather,
And the things that life can bring.

Their colors all mismatched,
Yet the bond shines so bright,
In the warmth of the sunlight,
They hold on, pure delight.

Each thread tells a story,
Of a tumble and a spin,
With a laugh, a little twist,
That makes our heads just spin.

Forged in chaos, laughter,
These threads are made to last,
Bound by trust and mischief,
Their friendship unsurpassed.

Filigree of Friendship

In a world of jumbled threads,
We wear our quirks like crowns.
With laughter as the glue,
Our joy spins round like clowns.

Each mishap we embrace,
Like socks that never match.
We weave our stories sweet,
In a tapestry of scratch.

A loaf of bread, a rhyme,
We trade our silly jokes.
With every twist and turn,
We're just a bunch of folks.

So let's attach our tales,
With knots of goofy cheer.
In this grand design of life,
We'll never disappear!

Vows in the Loop

Two silly hearts entwined,
In circles round we go.
With vows of snacks and puns,
Our love is quite the show.

We dance in funny steps,
Like penguins on the glide.
With giggles in each leap,
We take this wacky ride.

Wrapped up in our own charms,
With every loop we make.
The chaos and the cracks,
Are just the fun we break.

So here's to vows we share,
In this perfectly looped way.
With laughter as our guide,
Let's seize the silly day!

Patterns of the Heart

In patches bright and bold,
Our hearts do weave and sway.
With puns that make us grin,
We'll stitch this quilt today.

Like mismatched socks we wear,
Our colors clash just right.
Each pattern spins a tale,
In laughter's pure delight.

Through loops and funny twists,
We dance a quirky reel.
In every twist that binds,
Our friendship's all too real.

So let's embrace the funny,
In this fabric of our lives.
With joy as our free thread,
In laughter love survives!

Unity Unveiled

In this merry jigsaw,
We fit in strange designs.
With laughter as our key,
We unlock all the signs.

Silly puzzles we solve,
In patterns that are bright.
With every little quirk,
We bring the world to light.

Each piece a bit absurd,
Yet crucial to the whole.
In this dance of chaos,
We find our common soul.

Together we're a force,
In this wacky parade.
With unity unveiled,
We've got an endless charade!

Melodies of Interwoven Lives

In the dance of daily life, we play,
Laughing at hurdles that come our way.
With each twist and turn, we take a leap,
Funny tales woven in stories so deep.

A sock lost to the laundry's grasp,
Hilarious moments—oh, how they clasp.
Like mismatched shoes on a busy street,
We find the joy in the oddities sweet.

Echoes of laughter fill up the air,
Chasing each other, we've not a care.
Life's a melody, quirky and bright,
Composed of joys that soar like a kite.

So here we are, all tied and spun,
In the game of life, we've all had fun.
Each thread connects us, wild and bold,
Funny stories in the tapestry told.

Twilight Ties

As the sun dips low, our ties appear,
In shadows we dance, sharing a cheer.
A sandwich shared with a grin so wide,
Together we laugh, no need to hide.

The cat chases lights like a wild spree,
Jumping in circles, oh what a glee!
While we sit back with popcorn in hand,
Life's funny quirks are simply grand.

Twilight casts spells, in friendship we trust,
Each goofy moment, a must, a must.
Wrapped in ties that shimmer and glow,
In our little world, the laughter will flow.

So let's celebrate the moments we live,
With chuckles and giggles, there's joy to give.
In twilight's embrace, we find our bliss,
A bond that's so funny, we can't help but miss!

Echoing Strength

Beneath the laughter, a strength resides,
Friendship unbreakable, a fun-filled ride.
With silly faces and ridiculous puns,
We stand together, victorious runs.

Like coffee that spills on a brand new shirt,
We laugh at our woes, despite any hurt.
Each echoing giggle adds volume and cheer,
In our web of joy, we hold each one dear.

Through trials and gaffes, we find our way,
Spinning our tales in hues of gray.
Strong like a tether, yet light like a feather,
Together we dance through all sorts of weather.

For in this world, as odd as it may seem,
Our bond is the glue that stays like a dream.
With laughter as fuel, we conquer the day,
Echoing strength in our own goofy way.

Whims of the Interconnected

In the web of fun where we all collide,
Like startled squirrels, we scamper and glide.
With jokes that fly over hedges and walls,
Laughter connects us through all our calls.

A mishap here and a blunder there,
We stitch together moments without a care.
With whimsy and wit, we tackle the task,
In the wacky journey, there's no need to ask.

Tangled in tales, oh what a delight,
From absurd mishaps to sheer silly sight.
Each moment a thread in this happy embrace,
Interconnected, we pace our race.

So here's to the quirks that make life sublime,
With laughter our rhythm, we'll dance through time.
Embracing the odd, we flourish and flow,
In a world full of whim, let our giggles grow!

Mosaic of Soulful Entanglements

In a jumble, I lost my shoe,
But found a key, or maybe two.
A dance of luck, a twist of fate,
My mismatched pair will have to wait.

A necklace here, a bracelet there,
My tangled hair, a wild affair.
With laughter lines and silly frowns,
We forge our bonds while spinning round.

A friendship formed from silly jokes,
Like socks that hide from playful folks.
In every twist, a story we weave,
As tangled souls, we madly believe.

A patchwork quilt of blissful glee,
With every knot, more laughs for me.
So here we sit, with hearts so wide,
Our merry bonds, we wear with pride.

Adornments of Fate's Design

A quirky hat, a tie askew,
In fashion's game, it's me and you.
A shoelace tied to someone's ring,
Oh, what a sight, the joy it brings!

With mismatched socks and cheerful grins,
We wade through life on silly whims.
A charm bracelet, loud and bright,
Its jingles echo through the night.

A crown of flowers, or maybe cheese,
In our odd style, we aim to please.
Life's silly dance, like grand ballet,
With laughter trailing all the way.

Beneath the stars, we twirl and sway,
In our odd outfits, we'll seize the day.
Together draped in chia seeds,
Adornments born from joyful deeds.

The Luminous Trail of Affection

A flashlight beam on candy trails,
Where glowing hearts leave silly tales.
Gumdrops stuck to shoes of fate,
A sticky love we debate and rate.

Each giggle sparkles like the sun,
In our little world, we've only begun.
A trail of lights, like fireflies,
Our zany path where laughter flies.

With every wink, the world's a stage,
We perform as clowns, with love to gauge.
Our sense of humor a radiant guide,
Illuminating joy, side by side.

Together we shine, a dazzling pair,
With goofy antics that fill the air.
On this glowing trail, we roam free,
In a dance of love and hilarity.

Metallurgical Musings on Togetherness

Two spoons dance in the crowded drawer,
Clatters of silver, oh, what a score!
A glimmer here, a sparkle there,
The clang of friendship rings through the air.

In pots and pans, we create a song,
Our culinary tales, both weird and strong.
A fork and knife, in a comical fight,
Laughing through meals, from morning to night.

A metallic hug, wrapped tight and bold,
Crinkling laughter like stories told.
Our shiny bonds, like steel at play,
In this kitchen, we'll dance away.

So here's to all the spoons and blades,
In the kitchen of life, our joy cascades.
With every clang, a note we write,
In the symphony of togetherness, we unite.

Security in Solidarity

When friendship's locks are tight and strong,
We laugh at troubles, sing our song.
Together we can face the night,
In silly hats, we claim our right.

With every twist, our lives align,
Like tangled wires, we're doing fine.
Lost keys? No way, we'll just not care,
With silly faces, we share a stare.

In jest we build our tower tall,
A fortress made of humor's call.
Locked in laughter, we won't implode,
Our goofy pact, the perfect code.

So here's to bonds that never fade,
In quips and jokes, our plans are laid.
No need for keys or fancy locks,
Just chuckles shared 'round our paradox.

Forged Connections

In clinks and clanks, our laughter flows,
The more we jest, the more it grows.
Welded friends with hearts of gold,
Each punchline, a coil to hold.

We trip on words, our humor's flair,
Creating chains without a care.
A tangled mesh of joy and glee,
Forged in friendship's clumsy spree.

When puns collide, sparks fly anew,
Our bond becomes an oddball crew.
Linked like socks that missed the wash,
We twirl through life with whims and posh.

So let's toast to our quirky tie,
With every laugh, we reach the sky.
Connections forged in jest and fun,
Shiny links bright as the sun.

Allure of Intertwining Paths

As we wander through this world so wide,
Our paths entangle like shoes that slide.
With each misstep, a tale unfolds,
In twisted fables that fate beholds.

We zigzag through the quirks of life,
Dodging drama, avoiding strife.
In every twist, a giggle born,
Unraveling troubles, we're never worn.

Like pretzels shaped by hands so bold,
Our knots of laughter never cold.
In jumbles of joy, we're never lost,
For every path, we share the cost.

So here's to routes that weave and wend,
For laughing lives, there's no end.
In every loop, a smile we'll see,
Intertwined, we dance so free.

Symphony of the Linked

In this orchestra of clinks and clatters,
Our laughter sings, the joy just scatters.
Each note a bond, eccentric and bright,
Together we play from day to night.

With rusty hinges, we'll make a tune,
A raucous sound like a cartoon.
In playful keys, we joke and rhyme,
Creating a masterpiece in no time.

Our symphony may not stay in tune,
But we groove along like a merry loon.
In tangled rhythms, we wobble and sway,
Together we'll dance, come what may.

So let's raise a glass, a toast to the fun,
In linked adventures, we're never done.
With every beat, our spirits soar,
A symphony crafted forevermore.

Lattice of Love

In a garden tangled and wild,
Grows a joy that's anything but mild.
A vine that laughs, a flower that sings,
Caught up in rhythm, they flutter their wings.

Petals wrapped round a garden hose,
Wiggling with glee, as the laughter grows.
They chase the bees, with silly delight,
Dancing in circles, from morning till night.

A rake joins in, it thinks it can play,
Swinging its handle, as kids shout hooray!
They prance and they twist, in a comedic show,
It's a chaotic ballet, in the yard below.

Chronicles of Ties

Tangled threads on laundry day,
Socks conspire in a comical way.
One's in a twist, another in knots,
The pants just laugh, they've got all the spots.

A friendship formed 'tween a shirt and a shoe,
'Oh why did they spin? This isn't our cue!'
With each tumble, a giggle erupts,
As static and static cling become their disrupts.

The dryer hums songs, a tune oh-so-cheer,
It's a wild party, come join if you dare!
In this fabric realm, the laughter won't cease,
They're bound by the spin, and the chaos releases.

Inextricable Patterns

In the quilt of life, we stitch and we sew,
Threads intertwine, oh where will they go?
A patchwork of laughter, some snags here and there,
With a tickle and tug, it's a comical affair.

Twisted up yarn, a cat's favorite toy,
Knots started tangled, no need for the ploy.
As it rolls and it tumbles, the furballs take flight,
They dance with the chaos, a hilarious sight.

A spoon joins the fray, it thinks it's a game,
Spinning and twirling, it's part of the fame.
When life gets too serious, embrace the strange,
For in all of this mess, there's magic to change.

Legacies of Light

In a world of bulbs that flicker and dance,
They share a sparkle, a luminous chance.
A bulb that's dim, with a wink and a smile,
Joins up with a flame, to light up the aisle.

A chandelier giggles, with crystals that sway,
'Join me, my friends, let's play in the ray!'
As shadows chase shadows, the room is aglow,
A festival of brightness, in a comedic show.

From strings of bright fairy lights, laughter takes flight,
'Take that, my dear switch, you can't dim our light!'
In hues of pink and splashes of blue,
Together they shine, creating joy anew.

Gleaming Threads of Unity

In a room full of laughter, we all come together,
Link after link, we're light as a feather.
With jokes that are silly and puns that delight,
Our bonds are so strong, they stretch day and night.

Chasing my friend who's lost in the crowd,
He trips on a leg, it's terribly loud!
Yet out of the chaos, with giggles we twine,
Creating a tapestry, oh isn't it divine?

We fumble and tumble through days filled with cheer,
A chain of bright moments, I want to keep near.
When life pulls apart, we just laugh and we weave,
With laughter as glue, it's hard to believe.

So here's to the links, both silly and sweet,
In this chain of our friendship, we never know defeat.
With every mishap, there's joy to embrace,
Together we're strong, no one can replace!

Chains of Serendipity

Stumbling and fumbling, on paths we collide,
In a daft little dance, where chaos can't hide.
Each twisty adventure, a spark of pure joy,
Found treasures like belly laughs, oh boy oh boy!

A muffin that flew like a bird in the sky,
Landed right on your head, oh my, oh my!
Yet amidst all the crumbs, we gather and cheer,
With moments so silly, it's joy we revere.

Stuck in a chain of absurdity's grace,
Where pranks are the fabric, and fun's the embrace.
With stories exaggerated, oh do take a seat,
Each link, a giggle, makes life feel complete.

Through tangled connections and mishaps so bright,
We celebrate friendship in day and in night.
Each laugh is a clasp, our joy interspersed,
In this crazy chain, we are truly immersed!

Shimmering Bonds of Heart

A smirk from a friend, what mischief awaits?
As we join at the hip, just like chain link gates.
With pizza box battles and sauce on our nose,
Our connections are shiny, like diamonds that glow.

We swap funny stories, one wrong turn leads,
To laughter erupting and filling our needs.
Our hearts intertwine with each chuckle and jest,
In this light-hearted game, we are truly blessed.

A journey through chaos, but oh what a ride!
With mishaps like confetti, laughter is our guide.
We're gleaming with joy, like stars in the night,
Each bond is electric, it's pure delight.

So here's to these links, in moments we share,
With humor unchained, there's joy everywhere.
A quip and a giggle, we play our own part,
In this radiant web, we weave from the heart!

Ciphers of the Connected

In this tangled up puzzle, we each have a place,
With laughter encrypted in every embrace.
The jokes that we share are the keys to the lock,
Unlocking the fun like a well-timed clock.

A slip on the floor, a spontaneous fall,
With giggles erupting, we're having a ball.
Each mishap we gather, like badges of pride,
In this wacky adventure, we joyfully slide.

A hand on your shoulder just makes the day bright,
When we break into laughter under soft moonlight.
We're ciphers together, in games that we play,
Our unity's stitched in a comical way.

So let's weave our stories, with humor as thread,
Through the moments we share, our worries we shred.
The bonds that we cherish, forever will bloom,
As laughter's our melody, dispelling the gloom!

Entreaties of Solidity

Oh link so sturdy, oh link so bright,
You dangle and jingle, a wondrous sight.
Why do you clink when I walk through the door?
You'd think you were a dog, begging for more.

In every mishap, you seem to help me,
When I trip on my shoelace, you create a spree.
With a laugh and a jiggle, you don't let me fall,
Dear chain of mine, you're my best pal after all.

Oh links of iron, all polished and bright,
In a dance of disorder, you twinkle with light.
Each twist and each turn, you laugh in the breeze,
A playful companion that aims to please.

So here's to the chain, both funny and stout,
In laughter and chaos, we never choke out.
With every new jingle, you sing me along,
In this clanking symphony, life's merry and strong.

Depths of the Weaved

In the depths of the weaved, oh what a mess,
My necklace won't budge; it looks like distress.
With a twist and a turn, like a dance gone awry,
I'm tangled in laughter, oh my, oh my!

You curl like a cat in a sunny warm spot,
My bracelet's got style, or maybe it's not.
With every new knot that you magically make,
I chuckle and ponder, what mistake did I bake?

Each loop that you tie, it's a riddle of art,
Like puzzle pieces, playing with my heart.
You giggle at chaos, you thrive in the thrill,
Every jangled moment gives me a chill.

So here's to the weaved, both silly and bright,
In the depths of my drawer, you bring pure delight.
With your quirky entanglements, I laugh and I squirm,
Dear chains of confusion, you make my heart warm.

Celebrations of the Interlinked

In a fiesta of links, it's a party for sure,
With ribbons and bows, we can't ask for more.
Each segment's a dancer, in colorful glee,
Let's twist and let's shout; it's a jubilee!

You twirl and you spin, oh gleaming delight,
Each color's a wave, in the shimmer of light.
With links interlaced, it's a carnival cheer,
Join in the fun, let's give a loud sneer!

The clinks and the clatters, oh what a sound,
In the celebration of chains, we're utterly bound.
With every new loop, let's raise a toast high,
To the joy that you bring, oh my oh my!

So here's to the interlinked, oh what a sight,
A gathering of laughter, all dressed in bright.
With every new twist, may our spirits ignite,
In this party of links, we're dizzy with light.

Reflections in the Chain

In the mirror, I see you, all shiny and chic,
Reflections of laughter, it's profound and unique.
You glimmer and dance, a show of your flair,
With each little wink, you radiate care.

You beckon me closer, with tales of delight,
A shimmering whisper that lasts through the night.
As I twist and I twirl, in this metallic trance,
Your stories unfold, inviting a dance.

Oh chain of reflections, you mirror my glee,
In every bright link, there's a story of me.
With humor in every loop, you twinkle and shine,
A joy in the moment, forever divine.

So here's to the chains, both sparkling and merry,
In the reflections of life, we play, oh so cherry.
With every new shimmer that bounces our way,
We laugh in the mirror; let's dance and play.

The Dance of Unseen Bonds

In shadows cast by playful light,
Two links twist in a subtle fight.
They jig and jive, a laughter spree,
Bound together, wild and free.

Each connection sings a tune,
Dancing under a silly moon.
They giggle, clap, spin and sway,
Foolish friends in a bright display.

Forget the rules, they make their own,
Chaining fun with a happy tone.
Together they twirl through the night,
Creating joy, oh what a sight!

Links that bind with a wink and grin,
Whirling 'round in a joyful spin.
In this journey, laughter reigns,
Chains of joy that never wane.

Metal and Heart in Harmony

Oh, what a tale of steel and beats,
Clanking loudly with funny feats.
Each metal heart knows how to play,
Keeping rhythm in a quirky way.

With every clash, a joke is told,
Witty banter in the frosty cold.
They jive and laugh, a merry band,
Two souls linked by a steady hand.

Gleaming lyrics dance around,
In sync with joy, no frown is found.
Together they craft a silly tune,
A melody under a cheeky moon.

Forged in fun, unbreakable ties,
Where laughter lingers and never dies.
A symphony plays with a playful spark,
As metal and heart light up the dark.

Ties That Silver the Soul

In glimmering waves, the silver shines,
Creating bonds that cross the lines.
A twist of fate, a comic link,
Surprise awaits with every wink.

They tumble, trip, yet never break,
Fooling around for laughter's sake.
Jokes in their clasp, secrets unfold,
In shining tales of joy retold.

Each twirl and twist, a giggle shared,
With every clink, the heart is bared.
The silver sings as they hop and skip,
Crafting smiles on a joyful trip.

These ties weave stories, crazy and grand,
A playful dance across the land.
Stay connected, let the fun combine,
For silver ties spark joy divine.

A Symphony of Unity in Glistening Form

In gleaming forms, they play a tune,
A symphony under the bright full moon.
Pipes of laughter, strings of delight,
Unity shines, oh what a sight!

Together they play, no need for rules,
Making melodies like happy fools.
Harmonies echo, a joyous spree,
In shimmering links, forever free.

Each connection, a note in the air,
Their laughter echoes everywhere.
A rhythm unfolds with every chime,
Creating fun one beat at a time.

So join the dance in this sparkling land,
With unseen ties, let laughter expand.
A symphony of fun, forever warm,
In glistening forms, we transform!

Intricate Harmonies in Iron

A loop of metal, shiny and bright,
Its clinks and clatters bring delight.
Dancing together, a merry crew,
With every jig, they laugh anew.

Worn by a jester, proud and bold,
His tales of mischief, a sight to behold.
With every clang, the colors blend,
Creating chuckles that never end.

Spiral of Shared Journeys

We twirl and swirl, in circles we go,
A twist of fate in this odd show.
Each friend we tether, with laughter we bind,
In this merry ring, joy is defined.

From peg to post, we swing and sway,
An endless loop where we love to play.
With slips and trips, delightful falls,
In this silly dance, everyone calls!

Fabrics of Fusion

Threaded together, a patchwork of glee,
Every piece told a story, just wait and see.
With colors that clash, like socks that don't match,
In this quirky quilt, we all find our catch.

Stitch by stitch, we giggle along,
Creating a tapestry, playful and strong.
With laughter the needle, and fun as our thread,
Making mischief, there's no need for dread.

Jewelry of the Soul

Adorned in laughter, we shimmer and shine,
A necklace of giggles, how divine!
Each gem tells a tale, a tickle or two,
In this sparkling bunch, there's always room for you.

With bracelets of banter, a jingle so sweet,
Together we march, feeling the beat.
In this jewelry box, where smiles entwine,
We craft our treasures, one joke at a time.

Whispers of Interconnected Dreams

In a world where socks often flee,
A quest for matching, oh woe is me.
But every stray, still finds a mate,
In the laundry room, it's never too late.

A pair of shoes that dance at night,
Swap stories of mischief, what a sight!
With each new journey, laughter swells,
From lonely tales, adventure tells.

A jigsaw puzzle, pieces galore,
One sly cat thinks it's a score.
As gusts of giggles fill the air,
The pieces clatter, a wild affair.

A band of keys, each one a joke,
Unlocking laughter as they poke.
Together they jingle, round and round,
A symphony of silly is found.

Links of Light and Shadow

A paperclip that bends with glee,
Snaps like a spring, oh so carefree.
It holds the world, but in a twist,
Where chaos reigns, it can't resist.

A spaghetti noodle, long and thin,
It dreams of being a violin.
With sauce and laughter on the side,
In the pot of joy, they all collide.

A chain of balloons, all askew,
Floating high, oh what a view!
But one gets lost, drifts from the fray,
The others giggle, 'Come back, hey!'

A dapper tie with dots and stripes,
Worn by a man who dances types.
Each step a stumble, each twirl a fall,
A stylish disaster, he gives it his all.

Echoes of Endless Embrace

A bear hug given by too many friends,
Backs bend over as laughter sends.
A tangled mess of arms and glee,
Who knew affection could be so silly?

A quilt that's from a thousand seams,
Whispers wishes and forgotten dreams.
Each patch carries tales, both sweet and bizarre,
Handed down treasures, a stitch for a star.

Around the table, forks take flight,
Spaghetti twirls in wild delight.
Saucy giggles jump from plate to face,
Who knew dinner could spark such a race?

Old wallets bursting with memories stacked,
Stories trapped where laughter's packed.
They open wide with a jolly shout,
And from within, chaos comes out.

Threads of Connection

A spider's thread, oh what a sight,
Weaves a web in morning light.
Each dew drop clings with giggling cheer,
As bugs get tangled, laughing near.

The telephone cord in a twisty knot,
A game of hide and seek, oh what a plot!
With whispers mixed, confusion grows,
A giggle fits in the tangled prose.

Neighbors' dogs with a leash entwined,
Chasing tails, oh what a bind!
Their barks create a symphony loud,
Overlapping joy, they gather a crowd.

A dance-off led by kitchen spoons,
Clanking rhythm beneath the moons.
As pots join in with a raucous cheer,
Cooking up laughter, so sincere.

Woven by Time

A clock that ticks to a silly beat,
Marks the time with two left feet.
As hours dance like a rubber band,
Time wobbles on, oh unplanned!

Old stories shared, in threads so bright,
Looping together, a cozy night.
With every tale, a chuckle grows,
Like slapstick films from long ago.

A family tree, with branches wide,
Bears fruit of laughter, joy, and pride.
Each cousin's quirks redefined,
In bonds of whimsy, we're all aligned.

A calendar filled with fun and flair,
Doodles sprout in the empty air.
Every day's a chance to play,
Woven with giggles, come what may.

Echoes of Unbroken Bonds

In a clumsy twist, we laugh, we play,
Link by link, in a silly display.
Unyielding laughter, a tangled cheer,
Together we trip, with naught but a sneer.

Bouncing around, like balloons on a spree,
Our friendship's a chain, wild as can be.
Caught in a tangle, oh what a sight,
Wobbling together, we dance through the night.

Whispers in Metal

A whispering clang brings giggles near,
Linked in the fun, we've nothing to fear.
Our jokes fly high, like a kite in the breeze,
Bound by the laughter that puts us at ease.

In the kitchen, we cook up a spread,
With forks and spoons dancing, hope not to tread.
Each clatter a song, a comical tune,
In this metal ballet, we'll trip 'neath the moon.

Laced in Connection

Lace up your shoes, we're off on a quest,
Twisting and turning, we bring out our best.
A jumble of moments, a right merry whirr,
In the art of the link, we giggle and stir.

Each loop is a story, bizarre and absurd,
With laughter as loud as the flapping of birds.
We tie up our troubles in knots of pure glee,
As we lasso the day, just you wait and see!

Entwined in Grace

With a hop and a skip, we glide like ballet,
Twisted together, we frolic and sway.
Like a salad spun fast, with veggies galore,
Entwined in fun, we just can't ignore.

A pinch of the raucous, a dash of delight,
In this jumbled tango, everything feels right.
With a toss and a turn, the laughter's a chase,
Oh, what a whirlwind, all laced in grace!

Symphony of the Strung

In a world where links gleam wide,
A squeaky tune, the laughter slides.
A jingle-jangle, oh so bright,
With each connection, pure delight.

Tangled tales and silly knots,
A chorus sung from silly thoughts.
Bells and whistles, quite absurd,
In this symphony, we're all the birds.

Each link a note, a quirky twist,
Chasing dreams, we can't resist.
A swing and sway, the dance begins,
Rolling laughter, where joy wins.

Cups and spoons in playful reach,
Life's a song, let's practice speech.
Joined together, a silly spree,
In loops of fun is where we'll be.

Interlaced Stories

Once upon a tangle, oh what a sight,
Stories interlinked, day and night.
Hooked on giggles, winding around,
In this web, joy is found.

Fables whispered in every twist,
The truth, my friend, is often missed.
From rubber bands to paper clips,
Every bond has humorous flips.

Knitted tales of cats and mice,
Far-fetched dreams, oh so nice.
Patchwork friendships, linked we stand,
In every knot, a silly brand.

With each mishap, a laugh we share,
A fabric of fun, beyond compare.
Together woven, hearts will sing,
In this dance, we're all a fling.

Cords of Kindred Spirits

Bungee cords and stretchy ties,
The jump of joy, with silly cries.
Tangled paths and hiking trails,
Laughter echoing, never fails.

Yarns of friendship, spun so tight,
In every misstep, find the light.
With silly strings, we jump and play,
Bonding brightly, come what may.

Wrapped together in a loop,
A wobbly, giggling troop.
Through ups and downs, we share a laugh,
On this wild and quirky path.

Ties that bind, yet set us free,
In silly bonds, just you and me.
A dance of chaos, twirl and cheer,
With every knot, we persevere.

Sparkling Junctions

In every corner, sparkles flash,
Connections made in a zany dash.
Bouncing bright from here to there,
A whirl of giggles fills the air.

Zigzag paths and winding roads,
At each new turn, a joke explodes.
Funny faces and silly sounds,
In these junctions, joy abounds.

A flick and twirl of shiny chains,
Laughter tangled, joy remains.
Side by side, we leap and spring,
In this journey, we all sing.

So join the dance, and take a chance,
Life's a riot, let's all prance.
Between the links, let humor reign,
In sparkling moments, love's the gain.

An Alchemy of Human Connection

In a world so oddly spun,
Friends are precious, bear the fun.
Necklaces made of silly laughs,
Jewels found in silly gaffes.

We mix our quirks, a vibrant blend,
Like potion brews that never end.
One's a jokester, one's a sage,
Together we're a human cage.

When troubles come, we conjure glee,
A wand of wit, just you and me.
With spells of joy, we ride the wave,
Crafting memories, oh so brave!

In this alchemy, we shine so bright,
Sparking laughter, day and night.
A concoction sweet, forever spun,
In the cauldron, we are one.

Halo of Boundless Affinity

A circle formed of silly tricks,
Friends are like the best of picks.
We twirl in loops, a giddy dance,
Partners in an odd romance.

With every laugh, a comet flies,
Through cosmic jokes and quirky highs.
A radiant glow when we unite,
Our halo shines, oh what a sight!

Boundless bonds with quirky flair,
Chaotic thoughts hang in the air.
We giggle like there's no tomorrow,
Through all the joy, no room for sorrow!

So come, my friend, and grab my hand,
Together let's build jester land!
In this arena where humor reigns,
A laughter ring that breaks all chains.

The Fabric of Intertwined Horizons

We weave our tales with threads of fun,
Laughter echoes - the dance's begun.
Each yarn a story spun with care,
Stitching moments beyond compare.

In fabric bright, our colors blend,
We stitch a quilt, each thread, a friend.
Lively patterns, wild and free,
Together we make a tapestry!

The fabric glimmers in the sun,
Woven patterns, never done.
A toss of yarn, a twist of fate,
Creating art, we celebrate!

As horizons stretch, we find our way,
Through laughter's light, we seize the day.
A quilt of joy, a patch of cheer,
Stitched together, year by year!

Connection in Molten Metal

We melt our hearts in laughter's fire,
Alloyed souls, we never tire.
Silly sparks that fly around,
A fusion's joy is what we found.

In molten gold, our quirks combine,
Molding moments, oh so fine.
Each giggle rings like a smithy's bell,
Crafting joys, together we dwell.

With every jest, we pour our hearts,
In a foundry where humor starts.
We hammer out our shared delight,
Forging bonds, outrageously tight!

In this metal, laughter glows,
A sturdy strength that always shows.
In molten metal, we take a stand,
Creating memories, hand in hand.

Nexus of Touch

A jigsaw puzzle, we connect,
With missing pieces to perfect.
In every glance, a giggle lies,
Our quirks a charm, oh what a prize.

Tangled up in silly trysts,
With playful winks and gentle twists.
We dance in circles, round and round,
In this embrace, pure joy is found.

Like rubber bands that stretch and bend,
Each knot we make, we laugh and spend.
With every tug, a cheerful cheer,
Bound by each other, ever near.

Our fingers weave a story bright,
In every hug, we take delight.
With goofy grins and silly faces,
A twirling mess in cozy places.

Dancing in the Links

In a world of giggles and grins,
We bounce along like playful sins.
With every link, a dance begins,
Our feet in sync, do-si-do spins.

Like chain reactions of delight,
With every laugh, we soar in flight.
In this delightful chain of fate,
Who knew our bonds could be so great?

We twirl around with arms out wide,
Through every twist, we take a ride.
With chuckles echoing in the air,
The chains we forge are filled with care.

Imagine us on this merry spree,
Linked together, a sight to see.
With every step, we skip along,
In this weird waltz, we all belong!

Tokens of Togetherness

Collecting memories, one by one,
Each silly story, a ton of fun.
We clasp our hands, a tangled knot,
In laughter's grip, we find our spot.

A token here, a treasure there,
In every smile, a love to share.
With tokens bright, we play and jest,
In this collection, we are blessed.

Through ups and downs, we cheer and mock,
Our quirky tales like ticking clocks.
In every glance, a wink and nudge,
Together, we forever judge.

With tokens of joy, we race and play,
In this chain of giggles, come what may.
For every laugh, an even score,
Together, we can't help but want more!

Crescendo of Connection

With each heartbeat, we sync in time,
Unofficially, we form a rhyme.
In laughter's grip, we find our beat,
A merry bunch, we can't be beat.

Each twist and turn, a humorous plot,
In our silly dance, we lose the slot.
With every joke, our hearts ignite,
A crescendo grows, outshining the night.

Like marionettes, our strings entwine,
In a dance of joy, we feel divine.
With every chortle, a swell of cheer,
A symphony played for all to hear.

Together in sync, we rise and fall,
In this quaint waltz, we conquer all.
Our chains of laughter, a wondrous song,
In this merry realm, we all belong!

Meaning in Metals

In a world of shiny links,
I found a spoon that clinks.
It giggles when it stirs my tea,
And whispers secrets just to me.

A twisted fork once made a joke,
About the spoon, oh what a bloke!
They laugh while tangled in their fight,
Who knew utensils had such might?

I tried to fashion a bracelet bold,
But only tangled tales unfold.
With every knot, I lost my way,
Who knew metal had much to say?

Yet in this madness of the bling,
I hear the laughter, oh how it sings!
These gleaming chains, both wild and free,
Bring endless giggles just for me.

Enigmas of the Bound

What happens when you tie your shoe,
To a link that's twice the size of you?
You have a problem, oh what a bind,
And comedy's what you will find!

A dog once saw a chain so bright,
He thought it was a toy, what a sight!
He tried to fetch, oh what a mess,
Now he's the king of doggy stress!

Two friends once locked their bikes in place,
Forgot the key, oh what a race!
They hopped on one, oh what a fall,
Laughter echoed through the hall.

Yet in these binds of tangled fate,
We find the joy, we celebrate!
For though we're bound, we always strive,
To find the giggles and feel alive.

Rivets of Resilience

In a factory where laughter's loud,
The rivets dance, they're quite the crowd!
They bolt themselves to every floor,
And prank the workers, wanting more!

A hammer once played a boisterous tune,
While bolts were jiving around at noon.
They spun and swayed with zeal so grand,
Creating mischief by their hand.

I tried to start a metal band,
But lost my picks; oh, isn't that grand?
Instead, the screws began to glide,
And turned my workshop into a slide!

Yet in the chaos of this scene,
These rivets show just what they mean.
With strength in laughter, heart, and might,
They keep us grounded, day and night.

Chains of Familiarity

In the park where chains do swing,
Children slide and birds do sing.
But what if chains could talk and tease?
Their words would float on gentle breeze!

A swing once spoke to a fellow slide,
'Why do you give those kids a ride?'
The slide just laughed and took a turn,
In friendship's glow, they both did learn.

While merry-go-rounds just spin and spin,
They crack up jokes about the din.
Tangled up in childhood glee,
Chains weave stories endlessly.

And so in laughter, they all play,
In bonds of joy, just day by day.
Together they dance, both sleek and fine,
And share a giggle, pure and divine.

Kinship in Alloy

In a garage full of gadgets, we laugh and we play,
Each bolt and screw tells a story today.
From wrenches to washers, a metallic ballet,
We build silly contraptions, come join in the fray.

With rusty old chains, we swing and we sway,
Creating a concert of clinks on display.
Gather round, here's a joke, don't shy away,
In this scrap yard circus, joy finds a way!

A toolbox of treasures, oh, what a sight!
Each piece has a personality, a knack for delight.
We're just a bunch of nuts, under bolts of moonlight,
Turning work into whimsy, a purehearted rite.

So grab your wrenches, let's fashion a game,
In this alloyed assembly, we're never the same.
Laughter is the currency, fun is our aim,
Together we shine, not seeking for fame.

Tapestry of Togetherness

With threads of banana peels, we weave a delight,
In this fabric of friendship, we burst into sight.
A needle made of glee, stitching laughter tight,
We're crafting a quilt, oh, what a fun fight!

Here comes auntie's knitting, she's on a roll,
She swears her yarn's magic; it's got a soul.
Purls and humor, that's her primary goal,
In this tapestry wondrous, we're all on patrol!

Each stitch tells a story, each knot is a giggle,
As we snugly entwine, we sharpen our wiggle.
Life is a patchwork, let's dance and let's wiggle,
Growing together, that's a beautiful jigsaw riddle.

Our tapestry flourishes, a riotous sight,
With stripes of bright colors, oh what pure delight!
We fall into laughter, wrapped up every night,
In this fabric of nonsense, everything feels right.

Woven Dreams

In a world full of yarn, our dreams take flight,
With woven intentions, we joke into the night.
A tapestry of mishaps, oh, what a sight!
Together we weave, our hearts shining bright.

Every misstep is laughter, every loop a cheer,
As we tangle our lives, we hold each other near.
Knots of good humor, they conquer all fear,
In this quilt of our dreams, friendship steers clear.

The more threads we add, the funnier it gets,
Each color a memory, none of us forgets.
With laughter in stitches, life's most robust bets,
As long as we're together, we'll have no regrets.

So gather your fabric, let's weave something grand,
With love and laughter, by our own hand.
This patchwork of joy, together we'll land,
In a world of our making, let's make our stand!

Fables in the Link

In the kingdom of links, where the funny tales dwell,
Each chain has a story, who knows what befell?
A tale of a bicycle, caught in a spell,
Pedaled too quickly, oh, what a hard shell!

The hook and the loop danced a whimsical tune,
They laughed at the moon, it was quite the cartoon.
Jokes in the links, bouncing over the dunes,
In this fable of laughter, we're all buffoons!

The links hold us close; they jingle and jive,
Creating connections, we all come alive.
In stories of laughter, we thrive and we strive,
In this fable, dear friends, we're all in the hive.

So let's spin our yarns in this humorous link,
Underneath the bright stars, we pause and we think.
With chuckles and giggles, oh, we'll never sink,
In the realm of good friendship, let's raise a drink!

Shadows of Togetherness

In the dance of shadows we play,
A jumble of jokes, come what may.
With giggles that echo, we sway,
Together, forever, in a humorous way.

Laughter entwines like a vine,
Running around, which is just fine.
Who needs a map when you're lost?
Bumps are just laughter, at a small cost!

We hide and seek in playful delight,
Like squirrels on a mission, what a sight!
Chasing each other in the evening's embrace,
Dripping with laughter, it's a mad race!

In our folly, we share all the glee,
No rules to bind, just you and me.
With every chuckle, a bond we create,
In the funny shadows, we celebrate fate.

Metalwork of Memory

A light rustle, a silly clink,
Where memories gather, don't you think?
Jokes hammered out on this old steel,
With laughter and love, we all feel.

Bending the truth, like a metal twist,
Each grin and giggle adds to the list.
Crafting our past with silly finesse,
Who knew metalwork could be such a mess?

Tools of humor in a workshop's glow,
Each punchline chiseled, we laugh and flow.
Remember the time we dropped that keg?
The clang was so loud, we fell like a leg!

In the forge of friendship, sparks fill the air,
Turning mishaps into moments we share.
With every quirk, we can now relate,
In the metalwork of memory, there's always a gate.

Tethered by Spirit

Tighten the ropes, let's share a laugh,
Bound by shenanigans, we're a quirky staff.
Take this string, it's not what it seems,
Tangled up in our wildest dreams.

Floating like balloons in our crazy antics,
We navigate life with our strange tactics.
Connected by jokes and a wink in the eye,
No need for escape, we just fly high!

Together we tumble, bounce, and sway,
Like a dog chasing his tail, in a fray.
With every tug, our spirits ignite,
In the tether of joy, everything feels right.

So here's to the bonds, a playful embrace,
With laughter and love, we'll win the race.
Tethered by spirit, we'll never fall,
In this joyous journey, we'll always stand tall.

Resonance of the Loop

Round and round, the laughter loops,
A merry-go-round of bouncy troops.
With every spin, the giggles soar,
Creating harmony, who could want more?

Like a record stuck, we play the same joke,
In the resonance, like bubbles of smoke.
Each punchline prompts another cheer,
Still laughing hard, we want more beer!

In a rhythm of fun, we dance and twirl,
Embracing the chaos, watch it unfurl.
With glee in our hearts, and joy on the loop,
We find our place in this comical troupe.

So let's spin together, just one more round,
In the laughter of loops, true happiness found.
With every chuckle, our spirits will bloom,
In this glorious cycle, there's always room!

www.ingramcontent.com/pod-product-compliance
Lightning Source LLC
Chambersburg PA
CBHW070007300426
43661CB00141B/290